⮟ **W9-CNA-461**

# BASKETBALL: THE FUNDAMENTALS

## BRYANT LLOYD

The Rourke Book Co., Inc.
Vero Beach, Florida 32964

PHOTO CREDITS
p. 6, 7, 15, 16, 18 © Andrew Young; p. 9, 10, 19, 22 © Bryant Lloyd; cover, p. 4, 12, 13, 20 courtesy Beacon News, Aurora, IL

EDITORIAL SERVICES:
Penworthy Learning Systems

**Library of Congress Cataloging-in-Publication Data**

Lloyd, Bryant. 1942
    Basketball: the fundamentals / by Bryant Lloyd.
        p. cm. — (Basketball)
    Includes index
    Summary: Explores the basics of basketball, including the rules, origin, and necessary skills.
    ISBN 1-55916-226-0
    1. Basketball—Juvenile literature. 2. Basketball—History—Juvenile literature. [1. Basketball.]
    I. Title II. Series: Lloyd, Bryant, 1942-  Basketball.
GV885.1.L55  1997
796.323—dc21                                          97–8439
                                                     CIP
                                                     AC

**Printed in the USA**

# TABLE OF CONTENTS

# THE GAME OF BASKETBALL

Basketball is one of the most popular team sports in the world. The game is fast and exciting. Girls and boys and men and women play basketball.

Basketball is played on a court with a hard surface. In **regulation** (REG yuh LAY shun) basketball games, two teams of five players play against each other. They score points by throwing the basketball through a basket.

Regulation games are those played in tournaments or leagues or between schools. They are played by the official rules of basketball.

Do you want to be an accurate free-throw shooter? Concentrate on the basket, and imagine the ball going into it.

*Basketball is a fast game played on a hard, flat surface. Its popularity has spread around the world.*

# OFFENSE AND DEFENSE

A basketball team has a chance to score each time it has the ball. The team with the ball is the **offense** (AW fents). The team trying to prevent a score is the **defense** (DEE fents).

*One way the offense moves forward is by having a player dribble, or bounce, the ball.*

*Basketball players pass the ball to move it around, too. Here two players practice the bounce pass.*

The offensive team moves the ball by passing it from player to player on the offense, or a player may **dribble** (DRIB ul)—bounce—the ball forward. When a player stops the dribble, the player cannot dribble again immediately. He or she must pass or shoot the ball.

# HISTORY OF BASKETBALL

Basketball for many years was popular only in America, where it was invented.

The inventor was James Naismith. He was a physical education teacher at Springfield College in Springfield, Massachusetts.

In the winter of 1891, the college asked Mr. Naismith to invent an indoor team sport for his students. Mr. Naismith's new game was played with a soccer ball. The idea was to throw the ball into a peach basket 10 feet (3 meters) above the floor. The game became basketball.

*About the only thing Dr. Naismith's original basket has in common with a modern basket is its height: 10 feet (3 meters) above the floor.*

# CHANGES IN THE GAME

The peach baskets were soon replaced by metal hoops and nets. In 1894, a larger ball replaced the soccer ball.

The so-called 10-second rule began in 1932. It forced the team with the ball to cross the half-court line within 10 seconds or lose the ball.

In 1937 the center jump ball after every basket ended. Now the team that was on defense is awarded the ball out of bounds after a basket by the other team.

If a ball is held by two players from opposing teams, the official calls a jump ball. In the NBA, or National Basketball Association, the two players will be placed in a jump-ball circle to jump. In high school and college basketball teams simply take turns with ball possession.

*The player with the ball has 10 seconds to bring the ball across the center court line from the other team's half of the court.*

# BEING BASKETBALL READY

Modern basketball is a much, much faster game than the one Mr. Naismith invented. Basketball players must have **stamina** (STAM in nuh), the strength to run without becoming overly tired.

*Being able and ready to scramble for a loose ball is part of being a basketball player.*

*Running, jumping, and suddenly changing direction are all skills of basketball players.*

Basketball players must be able to change direction quickly. They must be able to move from side to side—in a **lateral** (LAT er ul) direction—as well as forwards and backwards.

Basketball players must also be able to stop quickly and move forward quickly from a standing start.

# CONDITIONING

Being basketball ready means being in good condition. Legs and wind are of major importance.

A good diet and exercise are keys for good conditioning.

Running can help build wind-strong lungs. Running also builds strong legs. Weightlifting can help build additional muscle strength.

Stretching helps keep muscles loose and less likely to be injured.

Any player's exercise program should be under the care of a knowledgeable adult.

Most shots taken at the basket are jump shots. Until the late 1940's, basketball players almost always took set shots. With a set shot, the player's feet were set—never left the floor.

*Stretching exercises help to warm muscles and prepare a team for its early morning workout.*

# GAME SKILLS

In addition to being in condition, basketball players need special skills for the game.

Being able to shoot a basketball with accuracy is a major skill. Good shooters often practice their shots daily, sometimes for hours.

Rebounding is another special skill. It requires jumping ability, strong hands, and knowing how to position one's body.

Quick hands and feet help basketball players with their special skills on both offense and defense.

*Practice won't make shooters perfect, but it will steadily improve their skill.*

# COACHING

A coach is the leader of a basketball team off the court. He or she is a teacher, planner, and **motivator** (MO tuh vayt er).

A coach teaches skills. He or she plans a way for the team to play offense and defense for each game.

*Basketball coach tells players what he expects them to do in an upcoming game.*

*Coach uses a player and a basketball to teach game skills.*

A coach also helps players be prepared for games. That means help with conditioning. It also means helping players believe in their ability and the ability of their team.

Coaches motivate. They make their players want to play hard and well.

# TEAMWORK

Coaches try to build teams with a positive attitude. A positive attitude is a feeling that, yes, this game can be won. Yes, I will play unselfishly. I will play by the coach's plan to win this game.

Basketball requires that each player know his or her role, or job. That may be to score or just rebound and play strong defense.

The best basketball teams have players who understand their individual roles. Then the five play as a team. That's teamwork.

For a hook shot, the player's left side is closest to the basket if the shooter is right-handed. The right hand—the shooting hand—is then protected from the defense by the width of the shooter's body.

*By hustling on defense, even one player can make all his or her teammates play better.*

# GLOSSARY

**defense** (DEE fents) — the team that is defending its basket

**dribble** (DRIB ul) — to bounce a basketball with the hand, palm down; the bouncing of the basketball by a player

**lateral** (LAT er ul) — a movement from side to side rather than forward or backward

**motivator** (MO tuh vayt er) — one who gives others a good reason for doing something and makes them want to perform well

**offense** (AW fents) — the team that is trying to score

**regulation** (REG yuh LAY shun) — refers to a contest or equipment that is set up or made according to the exact rules of the game

**stamina** (STAM in nuh) — the ability to continue hard physical exercise or play for long periods; staying power

*Good basketball players can get better by playing harder, even in practices.*

# INDEX